PREHISTORIC GREAT LAKES

AN ILLUSTRATED HISTORY FOR CHILDREN

JOHN MITCHELL & TOM WOODRUFF

for Dudley, Mary, Matt, Andrew, Patrick, Kelsey and Lydia

Suttons Bay Publications
301 St. Joseph, Box 361
Suttons Bay, Michigan 49682
231-271-6821
www.greatlakeshistory.com

The earth is a beautiful, blue and green ball spinning through outer space. Although there are millions of other objects in the universe, only our planet is known to host life. Today living things crowd the earth from ocean bottoms to mountain tops.

All life on earth depends on water. Most of the earth's water is held in saltwater oceans, which cover over two-thirds of our planet. Fresh water is far more rare.

The five Great Lakes contain the world's largest supply of fresh water, enough to flood the entire United States ten feet deep. The Lakes, named Superior, Michigan, Huron, Erie, and Ontario, shape the heart of North America with their familiar blue outline. People have enjoyed the wealth and variety of the Great Lakes region for thousands of years. Yet the Great Lakes are a brand new feature of the earth, the latest chapter in a story that began billions of years ago with the birth of the earth itself.

People, too, are newcomers to our planet, which has a long and mysterious past. Since earliest time, the face of the earth, including the Great Lakes region, has changed constantly, shaped by the forces of nature. The story of these prehistoric times lies buried like treasure in layers of soil and rock.

We find clues about prehistoric time in fossils, rocks with images of ancient plants and animals captured inside. Fossils show glimpses of life on earth at different stages in time, often revealing creatures unlike anything living today. Each fossil is a piece to the puzzle of the earth's exciting past.

The word fossil comes from the Latin word meaning dug up. Let's dig down through time and explore the mysteries of the prehistoric Great Lakes.

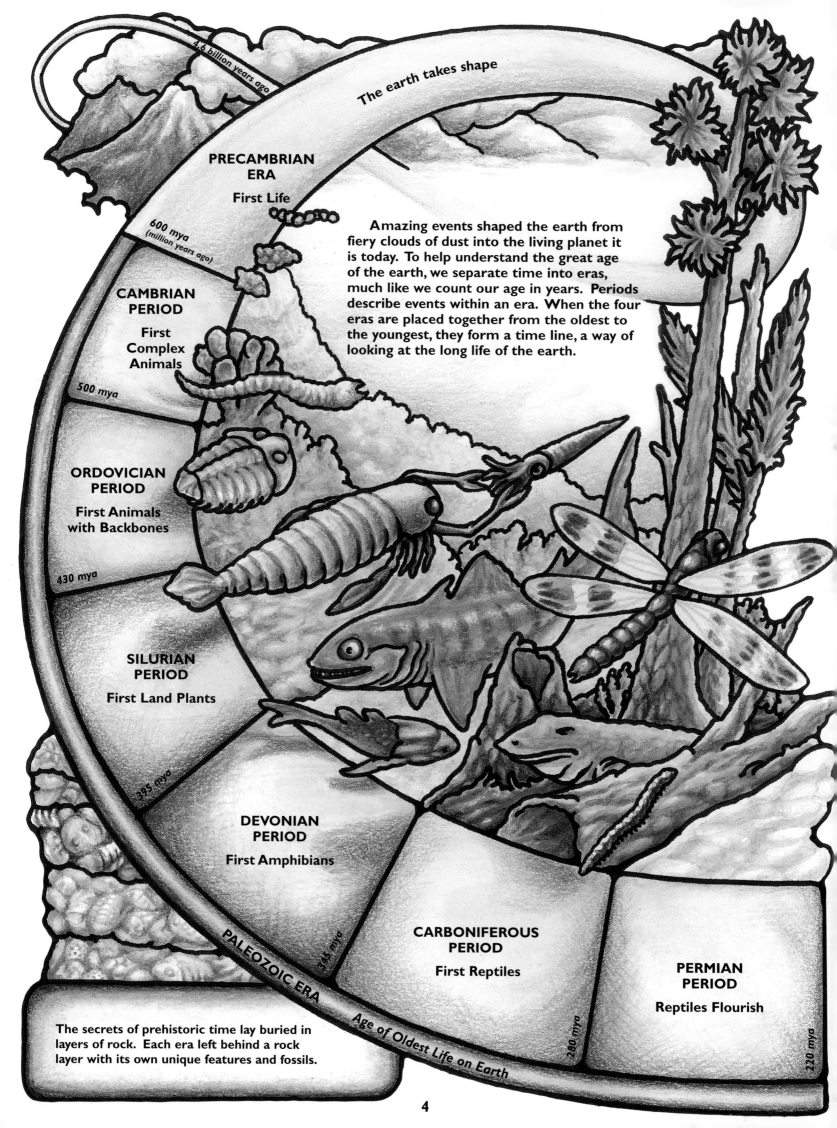

PRECAMBRIAN ERA

First Life

4.6 billion years ago

The earth takes shape

600 mya (million years ago)

Amazing events shaped the earth from fiery clouds of dust into the living planet it is today. To help understand the great age of the earth, we separate time into eras, much like we count our age in years. Periods describe events within an era. When the four eras are placed together from the oldest to the youngest, they form a time line, a way of looking at the long life of the earth.

CAMBRIAN PERIOD

First Complex Animals

500 mya

ORDOVICIAN PERIOD

First Animals with Backbones

430 mya

SILURIAN PERIOD

First Land Plants

395 mya

DEVONIAN PERIOD

First Amphibians

345 mya

PALEOZOIC ERA

Age of Oldest Life on Earth

CARBONIFEROUS PERIOD

First Reptiles

280 mya

PERMIAN PERIOD

Reptiles Flourish

220 mya

The secrets of prehistoric time lay buried in layers of rock. Each era left behind a rock layer with its own unique features and fossils.

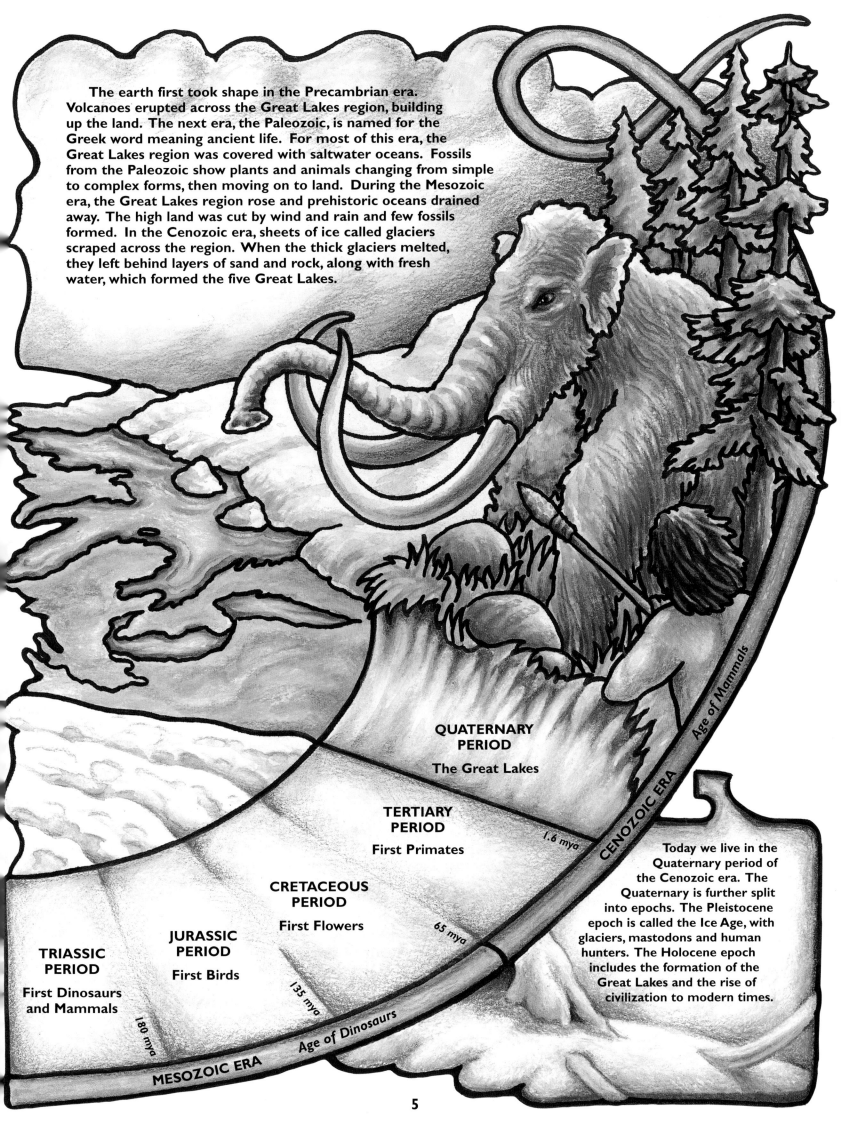

The earth first took shape in the Precambrian era. Volcanoes erupted across the Great Lakes region, building up the land. The next era, the Paleozoic, is named for the Greek word meaning ancient life. For most of this era, the Great Lakes region was covered with saltwater oceans. Fossils from the Paleozoic show plants and animals changing from simple to complex forms, then moving on to land. During the Mesozoic era, the Great Lakes region rose and prehistoric oceans drained away. The high land was cut by wind and rain and few fossils formed. In the Cenozoic era, sheets of ice called glaciers scraped across the region. When the thick glaciers melted, they left behind layers of sand and rock, along with fresh water, which formed the five Great Lakes.

QUATERNARY PERIOD

The Great Lakes

TERTIARY PERIOD

First Primates

1.6 mya

CENOZOIC ERA

Age of Mammals

CRETACEOUS PERIOD

First Flowers

65 mya

Today we live in the Quaternary period of the Cenozoic era. The Quaternary is further split into epochs. The Pleistocene epoch is called the Ice Age, with glaciers, mastodons and human hunters. The Holocene epoch includes the formation of the Great Lakes and the rise of civilization to modern times.

JURASSIC PERIOD

First Birds

135 mya

TRIASSIC PERIOD

First Dinosaurs and Mammals

180 mya

Age of Dinosaurs

MESOZOIC ERA

5

The Precambrian is the earliest era of time. It began when huge clouds of dust and gas swirled together to form a fiery ball called earth. Billions of years passed and the hot earth cooled. A crust like an eggshell formed on its surface. At breaks in the crust, volcanoes erupted and steam hissed from the earth's molten center. The air was poison. There was no life, anywhere.

Throughout the Precambrian, the Great Lakes area shook from the explosions of volcanoes. Mountain ranges grew where thick layers of lava stacked up on top of each other. Near Lake Superior, volcanoes poured out lava mixed with iron, copper, and other metals. The ancient lava cooled into a rock called igneous rock. Today, igneous rock is the foundation that holds much of the northern Great Lakes in place.

The Precambrian era spans most of the earth's life. During this time, the planet slowly cooled. The cooling caused steam held in the sky to fall as heavy rain. The rain storms lasted for centuries, sweeping across the young earth. The planet took on its general shape, holding both land and water.

PRECAMBRIAN

4.6 billion - 600 million years ago

The Precambrian is the oldest and by far the longest era of earth time. Four billion years passed while our planet changed from a hot, deadly place to one where life could survive.

In the Great Lakes region, tremendous rains wore down mountains and oceans started to form. Rivers washed sand, mud, iron and other minerals into the oceans, where they settled in layers on the bottom. On land, the air remained deadly and the sun's rays were too harsh for life. But something new blossomed in the Precambrian oceans, where life on earth had just begun.

The oldest fossils from the Great Lakes area reveal images of one-celled creatures called bacteria, the earliest evidence of life on earth. Other fossils have imprints of algae and primitive plants that used the energy of the sun to make their own food. Life forms of the Precambrian oceans were small but tough, and some relatives of the tiny plants and animals from this long ago time are still living today.

The Great Lakes region is home to some of the oldest rocks in the world. Around Lake Superior, igneous rocks are silent witnesses to the eruption of ancient volcanoes. Fossil rocks scattered about the region hold pictures of earliest life in the Precambrian oceans.

The origin of life on earth is one of the great debates and mysteries of our time. Gazing up to a star lit sky it is natural to wonder what brought us here. "How did life begin?" is a question asked since earliest record and repeated throughout human history.

Three hundred years ago, Native people of the Great Lakes region believed human life started when a woman fell through the clouds onto earth. Today modern religions teach that all life was created by the hands of a powerful God. Other people see life as an accident that began when conditions on earth became right for life. In time, each person decides for themselves the answer to this ancient mystery.

Fossil evidence demonstrates that once life started, it took on a force of its own. By studying rocks that contain fossils, we find that over time the size, shape and variety of plants and animals constantly changed. Early life moved from small, simple organisms to large, complex beings.

In time, each life form either adapted to the changing environment on earth or died off and became extinct. Fossils provide the clearest pictures we have of this succession of prehistoric life. Each fossil is another rock hard fact in the book about prehistoric life. Without fossils, we would know very little about the history of life on earth.

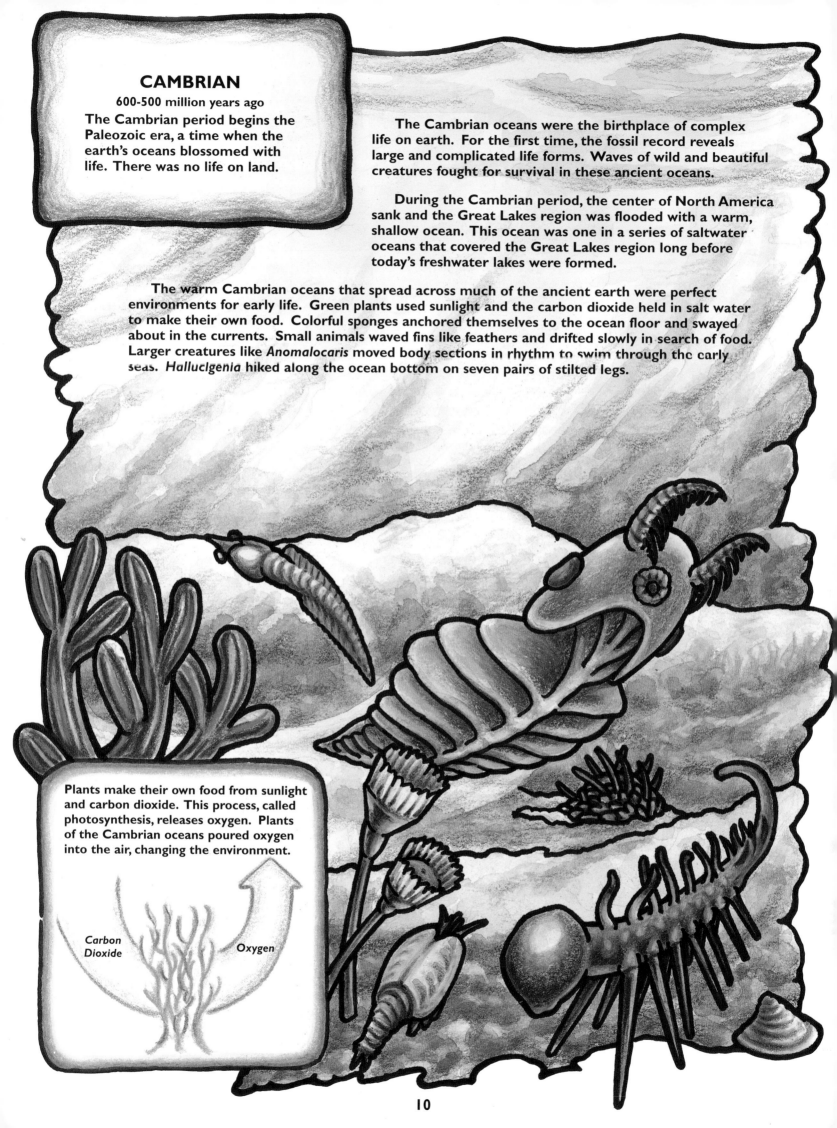

CAMBRIAN

600-500 million years ago
The Cambrian period begins the Paleozoic era, a time when the earth's oceans blossomed with life. There was no life on land.

The Cambrian oceans were the birthplace of complex life on earth. For the first time, the fossil record reveals large and complicated life forms. Waves of wild and beautiful creatures fought for survival in these ancient oceans.

During the Cambrian period, the center of North America sank and the Great Lakes region was flooded with a warm, shallow ocean. This ocean was one in a series of saltwater oceans that covered the Great Lakes region long before today's freshwater lakes were formed.

The warm Cambrian oceans that spread across much of the ancient earth were perfect environments for early life. Green plants used sunlight and the carbon dioxide held in salt water to make their own food. Colorful sponges anchored themselves to the ocean floor and swayed about in the currents. Small animals waved fins like feathers and drifted slowly in search of food. Larger creatures like *Anomalocaris* moved body sections in rhythm to swim through the early seas. *Hallucigenia* hiked along the ocean bottom on seven pairs of stilted legs.

Plants make their own food from sunlight and carbon dioxide. This process, called photosynthesis, releases oxygen. Plants of the Cambrian oceans poured oxygen into the air, changing the environment.

Carbon Dioxide   Oxygen

Worms that grabbed and pinched hunted for victims in the warm saltwater ocean. *Trilobites*, the first animals with eyes, crawled along the bottom using feelers to help find their way. The ancestors of today's lobsters sorted through the sand for a meal. Tube sponges and corals the shape of antlers grew in bright colors toward sunlight. A worm-like creature called *Pikaia* developed parts of a backbone, a feature many large animals would later share.

Throughout the Cambrian period, all life remained in the oceans. Nothing survived on the gray, muddy land. Rain washed small particles from the bare earth into the oceans where they settled to the bottom as sediments. In time, the mixture hardened into rock called sedimentary rock. The Pictured Rocks along the south shore of Lake Superior are an example of the sedimentary rocks formed long ago on the bottom of the Cambrian ocean.

By the end of the Cambrian period, many ocean creatures began to use minerals in the salt water to form protective shells around their bodies. When the animals died, their remains settled onto the ocean floor. Once in a while, the body of a plant or animal was buried by sediments before it rotted or was eaten. In time, the mixture hardened, creating a fossil. Sedimentary rock is the source of most fossils we find today.

Life advanced from simple to more complex forms in the oceans of the Ordovician period. The Great Lakes region continued to be flooded with a shallow ocean where many of the new life forms thrived. All through the Paleozoic era, North America lay closer to the hot middle of the earth, called the equator. The climate was much warmer than it is today. In this hot, tropical environment, the shape of Ordovician ocean animals changed often in the race to stay alive.

The first coral reefs grew in the clear, shallow water of Ordovician oceans. Reefs are made by tiny, soft bodied animals that build hard shells around themselves for protection. Millions of coral animals growing together in time formed rocks, underwater walls, and islands. These coral reefs provided food and shelter for other ocean creatures. Reefs became centers of ocean life.

Most animals of the Ordovician oceans protected their soft bodies with hard outer shells. Heavy shells were safe but slowed the animals down. New types of animals with backbones inside their bodies learned to move faster than animals with shells. Speed became a new weapon for survival.

ORDOVICIAN

500-430 million years ago
During the Ordovician period, over two thirds of the earth was covered with water, as it is today. Life was most successful in the shallows where land and water met, for here food was often most plentiful.

The way an animal looks depends on its genes, which are tiny chemical chains inside their bodies. Each link in the gene chain shapes part of an animal by telling it how to grow. Genes are the control centers for all life forms. When a gene chain is twisted or broken, it creates a new gene. A new gene makes the animal different in some way from all others.

Each experiment in life formed by a new gene is tested by time. Many new plants and animals die off quickly, for the change in their bodies is harmful. Others thrive for a while then become extinct. Only a few life forms are lucky enough to survive the challenges of a constantly changing environment and have descendants living today.

Ordovician organisms, called *brachiopods*, protected their soft bodies with hinged shells. *Graptolites* in the shape of spiders and badges sparkled in the sunny shallows. Ancestors of the octopus and squid scooted about the ocean floor, protected by horn shaped shells. Ordovician starfish looked and lived like their modern relatives, searching the edge of the living coral reefs for a meal.

13

SILURIN

430-395 million years ago

Life continued to flourish in the ocean that covered the **Great Lakes** region during the Silurian period. Fish with backbones were the most advanced animals of the time, and plants began to move from water onto land.

At the beginning of the Silurian period, the land in the center of North America remained lower than it is today. A saltwater ocean continued to flood the Great Lakes region. The ocean was shallow and warm and home to many new types of swimmers and hunters. Through most of the Silurian, the brown, dry land remained lifeless, while life underwater continued to diversify.

Coral reefs filled the shallow ocean covering the Great Lakes region. Their living rock walls continually grew towards the light at the ocean's surface, providing new habitats for early life. Ancient sea scorpions with spiked claws were great hunters in this coral world. The *Eurypterid* was a sea scorpion the size of a lion that prowled the Silurian oceans, searching the reefs for a favorite meal. Many ocean animals grew thick shells to defend themselves against the crushing power of the sea scorpion's claws.

For two hundred millions years, the cycle of birth and death left the old ocean floor littered with body parts. The debris settled in layers on the ocean bottom. Rivers draining the land filled the ocean with muddy water. Mud and shells mixed and formed sedimentary rock, with a fossil record of ancient times buried inside.

The level of the Silurian oceans continually rose and fell. Bays and lagoons flooded then dried. In the Great Lakes region, the salt left behind where ocean water dried up turned into a thick rock layer and was slowly buried. Today miners bring the salt back to the surface for use in our modern world. The salt we sprinkle on our french fries and popcorn was once the salt in the ocean water where trilobites and eurypterids lived.

14

The rise of fish during the Silurian began as they developed backbones. The *Pteraspis*, an early fish with a backbone, was one of the fastest animals of its time. It had no jaws, and fed by filtering water through its mouth. Later, fish were the first animals with jaws, which they used to rip food to pieces. Using backbones for speed and jaws for weapons, fish became the oceans' top hunters.

The Silurian ocean floor had a life of its own. Colorful plants and corals crowded the shallows. Trilobites, which were common in all the Paleozoic oceans, moved like insects in the underwater garden. A trilobite fossil from Silurian period is Wisconsin's state stone.

Near the end of the Silurian period, a few plants survived in the swampy areas where land and ocean met. Then suddenly plants began to grow all across the land, turning the brown earth green.

Three types of rock make up the earth's crust, and each reveals secrets about the prehistoric Great Lakes. *Igneous* rock formed in the Great Lakes region when hot lava from ancient volcanoes cooled. The lava contained many minerals, including iron and copper, metals which helped build the wealth of the modern Great Lakes. *Sedimentary* rock forms when particles held in water settle to the bottom and slowly harden. Layers of sedimentary rock from the Paleozoic era help shape the Great Lakes and carry with them a clear fossil record of ancient times. *Metamorphic* rock is made when material buried deep in the earth is changed by heat and pressure into something new. Limestone from ancient ocean bottoms is baked into fine marble, while wood from prehistoric forests is pressed into graphite, coal and diamonds.

The sedimentary rock formed during the Silurian period is important to the modern Great Lakes. The Silurian ocean floor hardened and survives today in the shape of a shallow bowl. The rock bowl is the basement and walls that hold much of Great Lakes in place. At sites around the Lakes, the edge of the Silurian bowl rises to the surface. The Door Peninsula of Wisconsin, Mackinac Island and the Georgian Bay Islands of Lake Huron, and the tall walls of Niagara Falls, are rocks formed from the bottom of the ancient ocean that once covered the Great Lakes region.

The Silurian ocean floor in time hardened into rock. The red area on the map shows where the Silurian rock rises to the surface and helps shape the Great Lakes.

It is a rare stroke of luck for a plant or animal to become a fossil. Most lifeless bodies are quickly torn apart and eaten by predators. Their remains disappear completely, crumbling to dust and leaving no trace behind. Fossils are created by accident only when a body is quickly covered by sediments and protected. Body parts are slowly replaced by minerals that harden into stone. The bottoms of lakes, rivers and oceans are the best places for fossils to form. The shape of shells and bones are most often preserved, while fossils of footprints and other plant and animal parts add to the picture of prehistoric life.

When a fossil is removed from a rock layer and brought in for study, scientists carefully separate the remains from the rock. A series of tests help determine the fossil's age. When the skeleton of a prehistoric animal is complete, it can be put together and displayed in its original living form. The frequent discovery of new fossils continually adds to the beautiful and complicated story of life on earth.

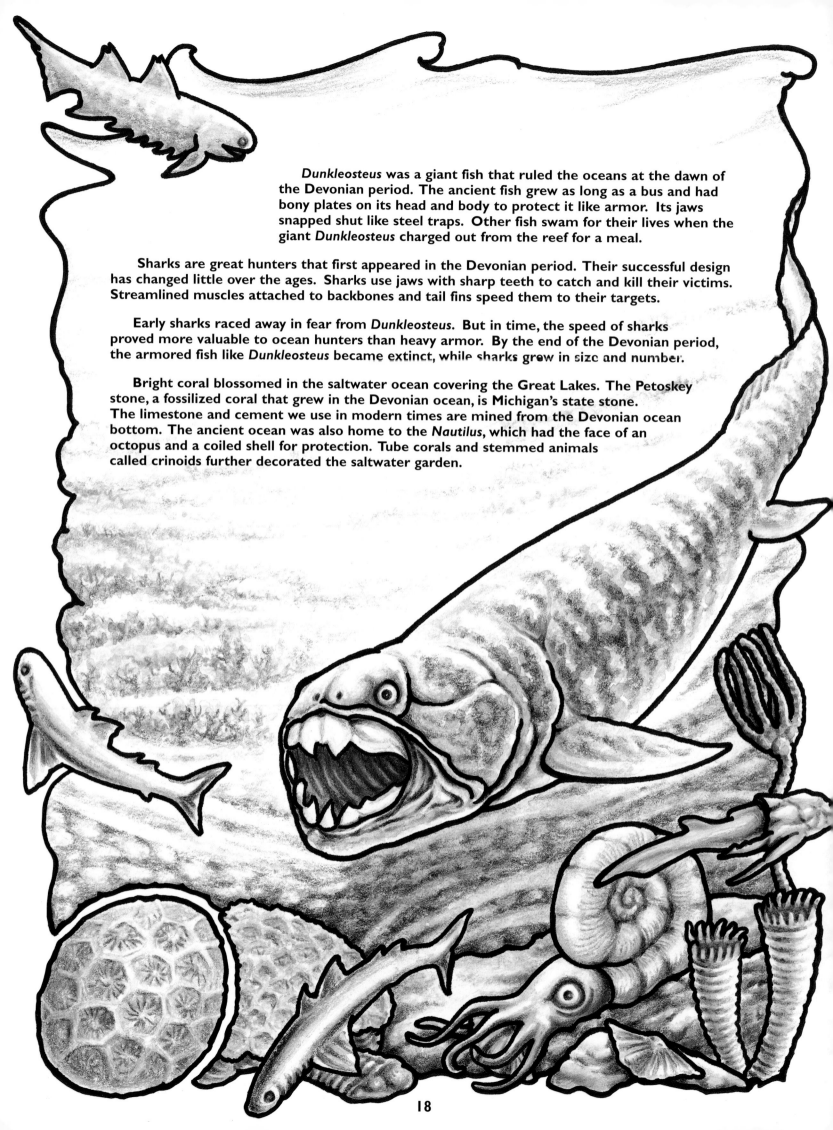

Dunkleosteus was a giant fish that ruled the oceans at the dawn of the Devonian period. The ancient fish grew as long as a bus and had bony plates on its head and body to protect it like armor. Its jaws snapped shut like steel traps. Other fish swam for their lives when the giant Dunkleosteus charged out from the reef for a meal.

Sharks are great hunters that first appeared in the Devonian period. Their successful design has changed little over the ages. Sharks use jaws with sharp teeth to catch and kill their victims. Streamlined muscles attached to backbones and tail fins speed them to their targets.

Early sharks raced away in fear from Dunkleosteus. But in time, the speed of sharks proved more valuable to ocean hunters than heavy armor. By the end of the Devonian period, the armored fish like Dunkleosteus became extinct, while sharks grew in size and number.

Bright coral blossomed in the saltwater ocean covering the Great Lakes. The Petoskey stone, a fossilized coral that grew in the Devonian ocean, is Michigan's state stone. The limestone and cement we use in modern times are mined from the Devonian ocean bottom. The ancient ocean was also home to the Nautilus, which had the face of an octopus and a coiled shell for protection. Tube corals and stemmed animals called crinoids further decorated the saltwater garden.

DEVONIAN

395-345 million years ago
The Devonian period begins the story of animal life on land. Animals followed plants and insects in their move from the oceans onto the shore.

Natural forces deep within the earth caused the Great Lakes area to rise during the Devonian. As the land rose, the ocean shrank and green plants quickly covered the emerging swamps and lowlands. Trees grew taller and taller in the fight for sunlight. Plants poured oxygen into the air, preparing the environment for oxygen-breathing animals.

Worms from the ocean crawled onto land and slowly changed into the first insects. One branch of fish, called lobe finned fish, developed new features to help them live in shallow water, where they could feast on the new food source. Lungs and nostrils let them breathe air. Fins became longer and stronger as fish used them to pull through the mud to even more insects. Fossils from the Devonian shows that, over time, the fins of these fish became the arms and legs of a new type of animal, called amphibians, which could live both on land and in water.

Amphibians spread across the land during the hot and humid Devonian period. But they were forced to return to the oceans to lay their eggs, which had soft shells and needed water to survive. Amphibians live on today as frogs, toads, and salamanders.

CARBONIFEROUS

345-280 million years ago

During the Carboniferous period, a thick, green forest spread across the Great Lakes region. The Carboniferous period is often further divided into the Mississippian and Pennsylvanian periods.

During the Carboniferous period, the Great Lakes area was a huge, hot swamp. Tall trees stretched toward sunlight and the first land animals, the amphibians, thrived on the wet and shaded forest floor. There were no birds to compete with fish and amphibians for insects. Giant dragonflies with wings two feet across buzzed through the hot air. Cockroaches as big as your shoes raced beneath the curling ferns.

Amphibians were the first animals to live on land. But their fragile eggs must be laid in water or they will dry up and die. Young amphibians live for a while like fish, then many adults change their shape and live on land. Even adults, with their smooth, fragile skin, need to stay close to water or they, too, will die.

Generations of huge trees rose from the Carboniferous swamp, then died and fell. New forests grew on top of old ones. A thick muck formed from the layer of dead plants. Millions of years passed and the plant layer was buried beneath mud and more fallen forests. Far below the surface, water was slowly squeezed out of the plant layer, and coal was formed. In other places, the ancient plants were pressed into a syrup called oil. Today large coal fields underlie areas of Illinois, Indiana, and Ohio. Pennsylvania was the sight of the first oil strikes in the United States. Now all Great Lakes states produce oil and coal formed from the plants of the Carboniferous.

By the end of the Carboniferous period, a new type of land animal, called reptiles, began to compete with amphibians. Reptiles had leathery skin and eggs with hard shells that held their own moisture. Reptiles were the first animals to be completely free from life in the water. They could roam deep into high and dry places where amphibians could not go.

Forces within the earth caused the ancient Great Lakes region to continue to rise during the Permian period. Oceans drained away, leaving swamps and dry land behind. Few fossils formed in the Great Lakes region.

Early life in the Paleozoic era was confined to the oceans. For a while, fish were the most advanced animals. Then amphibians crawled from the oceans onto land. They were forced to stay near shore, for their fragile skin and eggs could not hold water for long. The new Permian reptiles developed scaly skin and hard shelled eggs that could carry the water they needed inside themselves. Reptiles were well-equipped to roam the land when the climate became drier. By the end of Paleozoic, plants and animals had spread all across the earth, from ocean bottoms to mountain tops.

Dimetrodon was a fierce hunter from the new age of reptiles. Reptiles are cold blooded animals that rely on the sun to heat their bodies and increase their speed. *Dimetrodons* grew sails of skin and bones on their backs which quickly heated in the sun. On cool mornings and evenings, when other animals could hardly move, the saw-toothed Dimetrodon ate its fill.

PERMIAN

280-220 million years ago

During the Permian period, reptiles flourished and became the most successful form of land animal. The Permian is the final period in the Paleozoic era and a time when rapid changes in climate almost brought life on earth to an end.

From the Cambrian to the Permian period, life marched forward from simple to more complex forms. The variety of plants and animals steadily increased. The earth changed from a brown empty place to a living, blue and green planet. The Great Lakes area was a hot weather paradise where land and water met. It was summer all year long.

At the end of the Permian period, disaster struck. Volcanoes erupted worldwide and their smoke and ash blocked out the sun. The environment changed quickly. Oceans cooled and for the first time since life began, ice covered much of the land. The warm friendly earth turned cold. Rapid changes in the climate caused almost all plants and animals to died out and become extinct. Life on earth nearly came to an end.

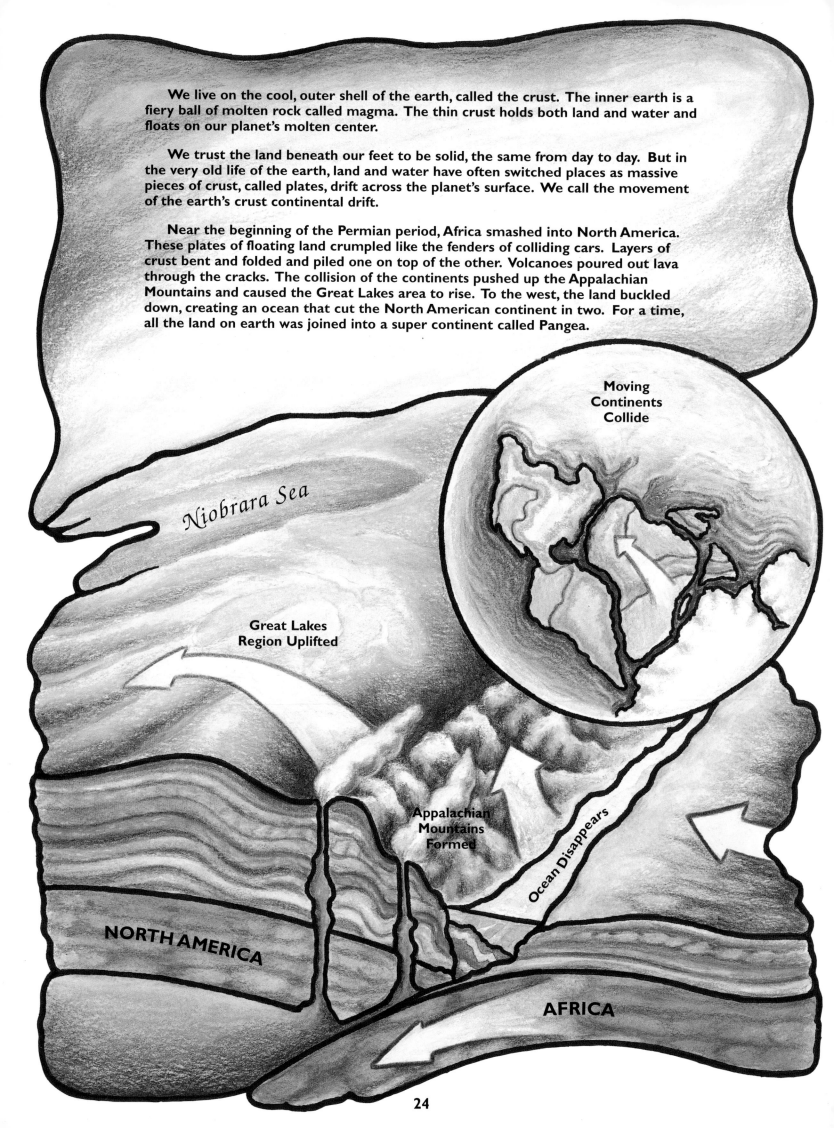

We live on the cool, outer shell of the earth, called the crust. The inner earth is a fiery ball of molten rock called magma. The thin crust holds both land and water and floats on our planet's molten center.

We trust the land beneath our feet to be solid, the same from day to day. But in the very old life of the earth, land and water have often switched places as massive pieces of crust, called plates, drift across the planet's surface. We call the movement of the earth's crust continental drift.

Near the beginning of the Permian period, Africa smashed into North America. These plates of floating land crumpled like the fenders of colliding cars. Layers of crust bent and folded and piled one on top of the other. Volcanoes poured out lava through the cracks. The collision of the continents pushed up the Appalachian Mountains and caused the Great Lakes area to rise. To the west, the land buckled down, creating an ocean that cut the North American continent in two. For a time, all the land on earth was joined into a super continent called Pangea.

Niobrara Sea

Moving
Continents
Collide

Great Lakes
Region Uplifted

Appalachian
Mountains
Formed

Ocean Disappears

NORTH AMERICA

AFRICA

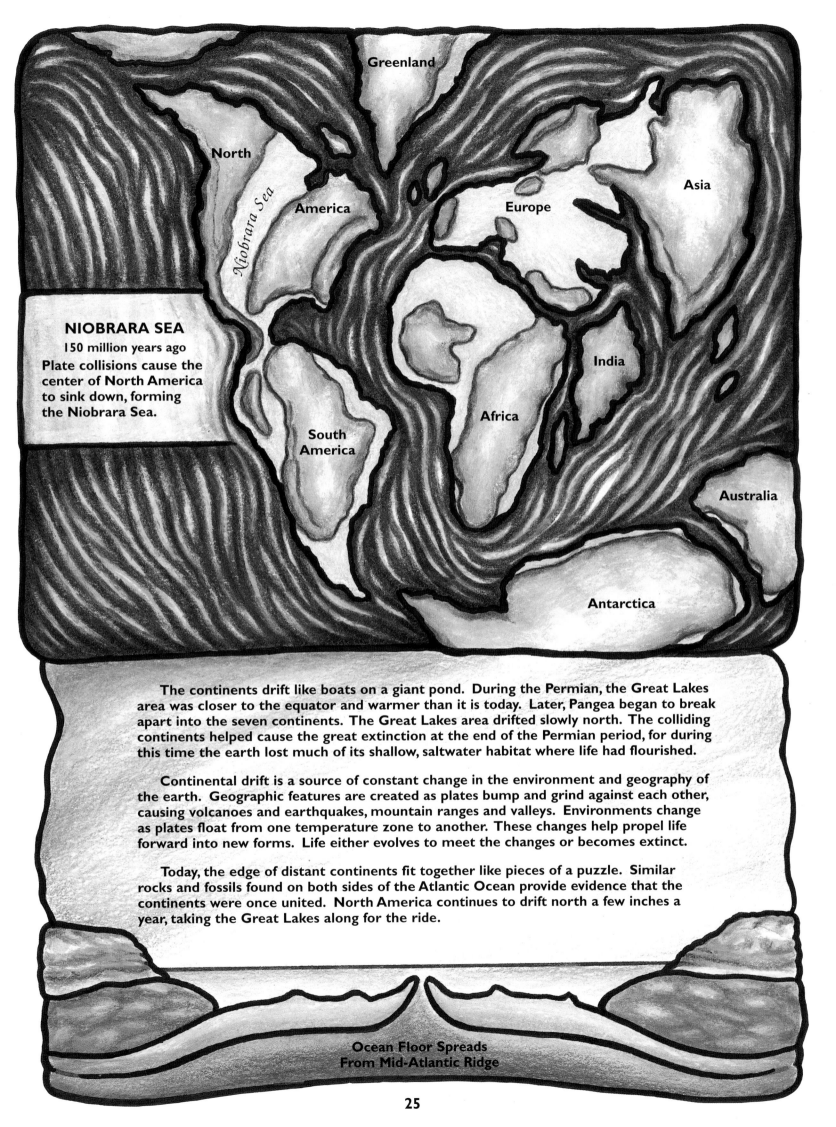

Greenland

North America

Niobrara Sea

Asia

Europe

India

Africa

South America

Australia

Antarctica

NIOBRARA SEA
150 million years ago
Plate collisions cause the center of North America to sink down, forming the Niobrara Sea.

The continents drift like boats on a giant pond. During the Permian, the Great Lakes area was closer to the equator and warmer than it is today. Later, Pangea began to break apart into the seven continents. The Great Lakes area drifted slowly north. The colliding continents helped cause the great extinction at the end of the Permian period, for during this time the earth lost much of its shallow, saltwater habitat where life had flourished.

Continental drift is a source of constant change in the environment and geography of the earth. Geographic features are created as plates bump and grind against each other, causing volcanoes and earthquakes, mountain ranges and valleys. Environments change as plates float from one temperature zone to another. These changes help propel life forward into new forms. Life either evolves to meet the changes or becomes extinct.

Today, the edge of distant continents fit together like pieces of a puzzle. Similar rocks and fossils found on both sides of the Atlantic Ocean provide evidence that the continents were once united. North America continues to drift north a few inches a year, taking the Great Lakes along for the ride.

**Ocean Floor Spreads
From Mid-Atlantic Ridge**

TRIASSIC
220-180 million years ago
The Triassic period begins the third era of earth time, called the Mesozoic. New super reptiles, called dinosaurs, first appeared during the Triassic, then ruled the earth for 150 million years.

Only a few plants and animals survived the deep cold of the Permian and hung on until the earth warmed up in the Triassic. The survivors took on many new shapes and features and fought for the spaces left empty by the Permian extinction. Reptiles quickly populated the land and began to search the air and water for new places to live.

Strange looking creatures are found in fossils from the early Triassic. One group of reptiles grew flaps of skin along their bony arms and sides and sailed from place to place on the wind. Flying insects no longer had the skies to themselves. The ferocious Cynognathus, a mammal-like reptile with coarse hair and jagged teeth, crept like a wild dog through the Triassic swamps, chasing and eating anything it could catch. Alligators and crocodiles hid in muddy pools and grew to twice the size of those living today.

Late in the Triassic, the most famous prehistoric reptiles, the dinosaurs, first appeared. The dinosaurs proved to be a very successful life design and soon spread across the land. Some dinosaurs were large, plant eating animals that walked slowly along on four legs. Others learned to run on two legs and became swift and deadly hunters.

Fossils from the Mesozoic era of the Great Lakes region are rare. Most fossils are found in sedimentary rock, which forms when debris settles out of water into low areas, then slowly hardens. The Great Lakes area during the Mesozoic was highland, part of the uplift of all eastern North America. Erosion wore away the area and greatly reduced the chance of fossil formation. The older Paleozoic era, the time when the Great Lakes area was lowland covered by oceans, has a clearer fossil record. However, areas near the Great Lakes are rich in dinosaur bones and footprints from the Mesozoic, and these fossils help create a picture of dinosaur life in the Great Lakes region.

The thick forests of the Jurassic were the perfect feeding grounds for huge land dinosaurs. The long necked *Diplodocus* could pick leaves off of trees seventy feet high. The giant *Stegosaurus* ate plants low to the ground, using its plated back and spiked tail for defense.

Wild rivers cut through the ancient Great Lakes highlands, carrying away soil and slowly forming deep valleys. Much later, the valleys would fill with fresh water to form the Great Lakes.

The success of reptiles in many habitats limited the rise of other groups of animals during the Jurassic. The first mammals appeared about the same time as dinosaurs, but they were small and forced to hide in the shadows for fear of being eaten. The new mammals had one advantage over reptiles, for they could control their own body temperature and stay fast and active at all times. Jurassic mammals crept out on cool nights, when their reptile enemies slowed, stealing an occasional dinosaur egg for a meal.

Bones, the hard parts of animals, are most often preserved as fossils. Soft parts usually rot before fossilization occurs. Bones are important to the study of prehistoric life on earth.

Dinosaur bones from the Jurassic help experts rebuild the animals from the frame out. The hip bones of the slow *Stegosaurus (left)* are like a lizard's, while the hips of fast, two legged dinosaurs *(right)* are more like those of birds.

Dinosaurs were the first animals to walk on two feet. Many two legged dinosaurs were fast and intelligent predators. Walking upright gave dinosaurs the chance to try new uses for their arms. During the Jurassic, one group of dinosaurs slowly changed arms into feathered wings and became new animals – birds.

The feathered *Archaeopteryx* is a link between dinosaurs and modern birds. It had teeth in its jaws, a long bony tail, and claws on its hands like a reptile, but its arms had become feathered wings. *Archaeopteryx* was a poor flyer, clawing its way up trees then gliding from place to place. But from these clumsy beginnings came all the beautiful birds of flight we know today.

Mammals learned to avoid being eaten by hungry dinosaurs. They hid high in the trees and dug tunnels deep in the ground. They stored away food for the times it was too dangerous to leave their homes.

CRETACEOUS

135-65 million years ago

Specialized branches of dinosaurs filled the earth with creatures unlike any others living before or since. Flowers and trees with leaves gave the plant world a modern look.

Reptiles filled the land, air, and water during the Cretaceous period. They prospered by adapting well to the many different living conditions on earth. Dinosaurs standing on four stout legs grew to be the largest land animals ever. Smaller reptiles stretched leathery flaps from their arms and legs and soared on currents of air. Other reptiles crawled into the ocean, where their arms and legs slowly evolved back into flippers.

During the long reign of the dinosaurs, North America was split down the middle by the Niobrara Sea. The Great Lakes area was the high, stable center of the continent that rose to form part of the Niobrara's eastern shore. Although the Great Lakes area is poor in dinosaur fossils, the best dinosaur fossils ever found come from the west shore of the ancient Niobrara Sea. The fossils prove that North America was once home to many dinosaurs and other famous reptiles. *Plesiosaurs* swam in the shallows, their long necks ready to reach for a meal. *Pterosaurs* sailed above, looking for fish close to the surface. Giant land animals like *Brachiosaurus* devoured the rich coastal vegetation.

Tyrannosaurus Rex and other meat eaters rested in the woods until hunger woke them. Triceratops grew three sharp horns on its head in hopes that packs of predators would look for something easier to eat. Ichthyosaurs lived much like today's dolphin, speeding through the water with powerful flips of their tails. The beautiful flowering plants first appeared and herds of dinosaurs learned to eat their soft, sweet petals. Pterosaurs and feathered birds fought for control of the skies.

Throughout their 150 million year history, dinosaurs adapted to changing conditions on earth. Continents drifted, climates changed, yet dinosaurs continued to live well in most corners of the world. New and unique dinosaurs appeared throughout the Cretaceous. Other reptiles ruled the oceans and fought for a share of the skies. The future of the hardy animals looked bright.

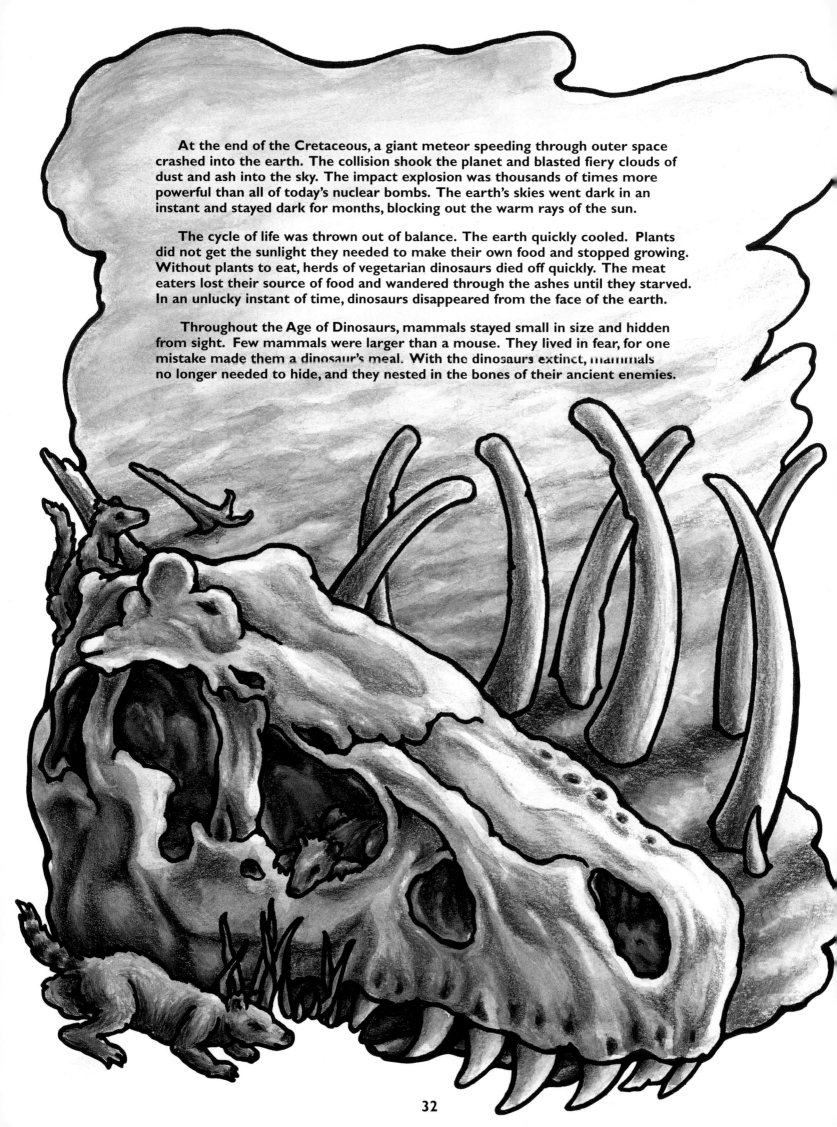

At the end of the Cretaceous, a giant meteor speeding through outer space crashed into the earth. The collision shook the planet and blasted fiery clouds of dust and ash into the sky. The impact explosion was thousands of times more powerful than all of today's nuclear bombs. The earth's skies went dark in an instant and stayed dark for months, blocking out the warm rays of the sun.

The cycle of life was thrown out of balance. The earth quickly cooled. Plants did not get the sunlight they needed to make their own food and stopped growing. Without plants to eat, herds of vegetarian dinosaurs died off quickly. The meat eaters lost their source of food and wandered through the ashes until they starved. In an unlucky instant of time, dinosaurs disappeared from the face of the earth.

Throughout the Age of Dinosaurs, mammals stayed small in size and hidden from sight. Few mammals were larger than a mouse. They lived in fear, for one mistake made them a dinosaur's meal. With the dinosaurs extinct, mammals no longer needed to hide, and they nested in the bones of their ancient enemies.

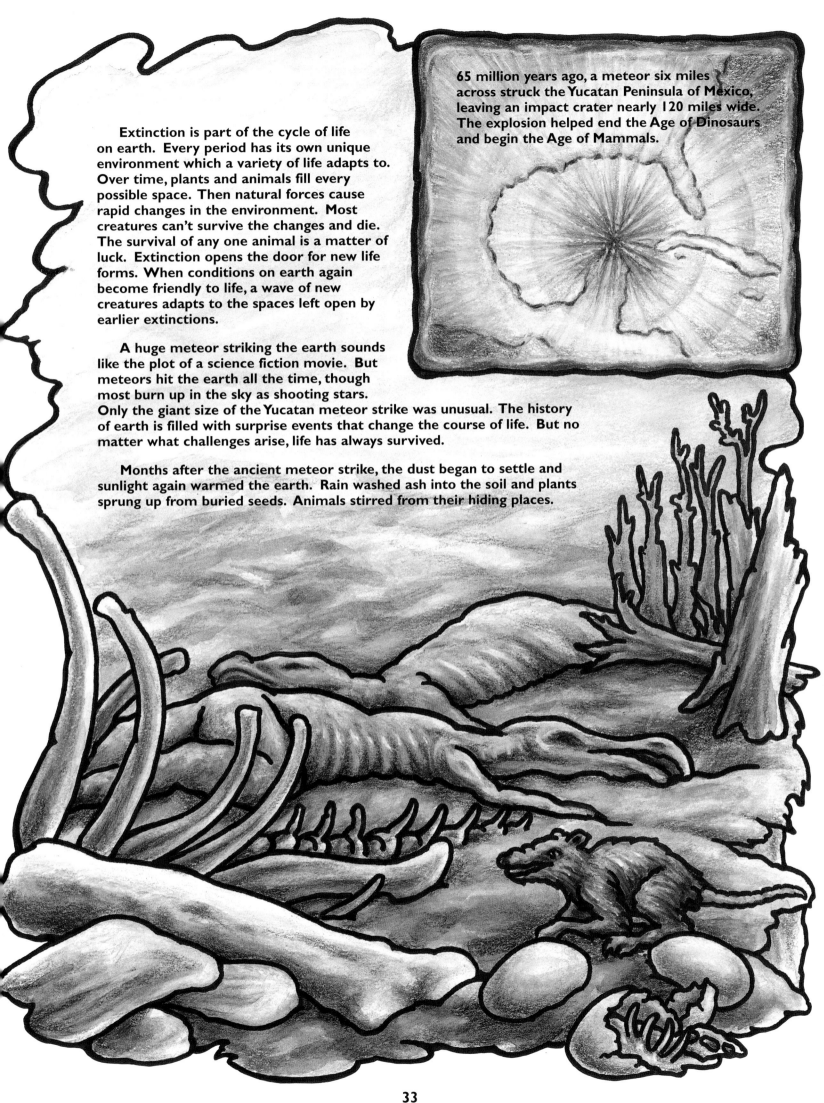

Extinction is part of the cycle of life on earth. Every period has its own unique environment which a variety of life adapts to. Over time, plants and animals fill every possible space. Then natural forces cause rapid changes in the environment. Most creatures can't survive the changes and die. The survival of any one animal is a matter of luck. Extinction opens the door for new life forms. When conditions on earth again become friendly to life, a wave of new creatures adapts to the spaces left open by earlier extinctions.

65 million years ago, a meteor six miles across struck the Yucatan Peninsula of Mexico, leaving an impact crater nearly 120 miles wide. The explosion helped end the Age of Dinosaurs and begin the Age of Mammals.

A huge meteor striking the earth sounds like the plot of a science fiction movie. But meteors hit the earth all the time, though most burn up in the sky as shooting stars. Only the giant size of the Yucatan meteor strike was unusual. The history of earth is filled with surprise events that change the course of life. But no matter what challenges arise, life has always survived.

Months after the ancient meteor strike, the dust began to settle and sunlight again warmed the earth. Rain washed ash into the soil and plants sprung up from buried seeds. Animals stirred from their hiding places.

Luck chose those who survived the dark days following the meteor strike. When the skies cleared, all the dinosaurs were dead. Mammals crept from their underground dens, where they had kept warm with coats of fur. Birds again filled the skies, while the skin-winged pterosaurs went extinct. Few of the once mighty reptiles remained. Some turtles crawled out of their muddy shelters. Here and there alligators hung on in shallow pools where they feasted on animals made careless by thirst. A new cycle of life began.

North America reshaped itself early in the Tertiary period. The western plate buckled upward to form the Rocky Mountains. The Great Lakes area was the stable center of the continent. The Niobrara Sea drained away and trees with leaves and flowering plants spread from coast to coast. The land took on a more modern look. A four seasons climate brought extremes in temperature, with hot summers and cold winters. Warm-blooded mammals, who kept their body temperature the same no matter what the weather, did best in the new land environment.

TERTIARY

65-1.6 million years ago

The Tertiary period begins the modern era of time, called the Cenozoic. Our planet and its inhabitants take on a more familiar look. Mammals dominate in the cooler climate.

With their enemies, the dinosaurs, gone forever, mammals grew steadily larger and more complex during the Tertiary period. Their sight, smell, and hearing improved and the animals became more intelligent. New and active mammals filled the four corners of earth.

Tall fields of grass spread across North America. The new plants fed growing herds of mammals. Early versions of camels, elephants, and pigs roamed the continent eating all they wished. Horses evolved from the size of a small dog into tall, powerful animals. One highly intelligent family of mammals, called primates, would in a short time rule the world.

QUATERNARY

1.6 million years ago to the present
The Quaternary period begins modern times on earth. The climate of the Great Lakes region was colder than ever before, and the period is often called the **Ice Age.**

Extremes of cold weather make the Quaternary period different from all other time periods on earth. Ice capped the north and south poles and stretched at times to cover one third of the planet. The sheets of ice, called glaciers, grew as more snow fell in the winter than melted in the summer. During several long cold snaps, much of the Great Lakes area was covered in glaciers over a mile thick.

Mammals were best suited for living in cold weather. Large mammals living at the edge of the glaciers adapted thick coats of fur. Mastodons and wooly mammoths, relatives of today's elephants, stored fat on their bodies in the summer, when there was plenty to eat. These fur-covered beasts were some of the first prehistoric animals of the Great Lakes ever to be studied, for their bones and tusks lay close to the surface, waiting to be found.

The mammals of the Ice Age were giants compared to their relatives living today. The lumbering *Megatherium* weighed as much a car and could bite branches off trees twenty feet from the ground. Early beavers grew to be the size of bears. Saber toothed tigers adapted special weapons to penetrate the thick fur of their Ice Age victims. A hinge on their jaws allowed them to open their mouths wide and use their eight inch teeth like daggers. The tigers patrolled the southern edge of the glaciers, looking to catch one of the giant mammals off guard.

Changes in temperature during the Ice Age created a cycle where glaciers advanced, then melted back, only to advance again. The sheets of ice were cold, quiet bulldozers that ground down everything in their path. The front edges of the glaciers stripped the northern Great Lakes area down to ancient rock, carrying with them huge quantities of stone and soil. Fossils lying near the surface were ground into dust. When the glaciers melted back, they left behind a thick layer of sand, gravel, and rock. The face of the Great Lakes area was changed forever.

Only fifteen thousand years ago, the last of the glaciers covered the Great Lakes area in ice. Slowly the climate warmed and the ice began to melt. A wide variety of animals moved on to land left open by the retreating glaciers. The story of the modern Great Lakes began.

The huge amount of water frozen solid in glaciers caused the level of the ocean to drop hundreds of feet. Continents once divided by water were now united. Land bridges allowed animals and humans from isolated areas to mix. Human hunters following herds of Ice Age mammals were the first people to visit the Great Lakes region.

In earlier times, meat eating dinosaurs and other top predators killed with built-in weapons like sharp claws and huge teeth. Humans, by comparison, were physically weak, with no claws, small teeth, and fragile skin. They survived not by speed or size, but by use of a new tool – intelligence. Humans did not need big teeth to kill, they made spears. They did not need to be large in size, they hunted in groups. Large Ice Age mammals, including mammoths and mastodons, could feed a roaming band of people for weeks, and the beautiful animals were quickly hunted to extinction.

A series of glaciers covered the entire Great Lakes region in sheets of ice over a mile thick.

Slowly the earth warmed up and the glaciers melted back north. Water filled huge valleys cut by the glaciers and formed the five Great Lakes. The Lakes themselves took on various shapes and sizes as the mighty glaciers retreated.

The early people of Great Lakes chased after the animals that grazed at the edge of the glaciers. Home was a bed of grass where the day's hunt ended. The tools and survival skills of the native people steadily improved. Hunters threw stone tipped spears with deadly speed and accuracy. Fishermen scooped whitefish and trout from the rivers with woven nets. Foragers knew just where to look for the best wild berries and nuts.

Small bands prospered and grew into tribes. Unique languages, customs, and traditions began to define the people of the Great Lakes.

12,000 years ago

10,000 years ago

The ability to communicate ideas set people apart from all other animals. Communication of ideas is the heart of custom and law and helps civilizations to rise. Through communication, people can agree on how to live together in peace and plenty rather than struggle alone.

The Old Copper Indians were one of the Great Lakes' first nations. They mined copper from the coast of Lake Superior at a time when glaciers still covered much of the region. The Indians hammered the bright metal into spears tips and fish hooks, knives and jewelry, then traded their works throughout North America. Three thousand years ago, the Old Copper Indians vanished, giving their cold country back to the hunters and the hunted. What happened to these people is still a mystery today.

By the time the familiar outline of today's Great Lakes emerged, Native American people had learned to grow corn. Planting their own food freed people from the daily hunt, and they began to settle in villages all around the Great Lakes.

4,000 years ago

1,000 years ago

A mighty forest spread over the Great Lakes region soon after the glaciers disappeared. Squirrels could race for miles through branches of tall trees and never touch the ground. Native people cleared patches in the dark woods and built their villages at the water's edge. They grew crops of beans and squash to serve with the hunters' duck and deer. Smoked fish and dried corn were stored away for winter. The Indians covered their homes in tree bark and animal skins. They chipped sharp edges onto stones they used for arrow tips and ax heads. Every family made their own bark canoes and travelled the many lakes and rivers of the region as highways through the forest. Children were taught the ways of the woods and the skills needed to survive in the natural world.

Native Americans of the Great Lakes region united into nations that lived in harmony with the forests around them. They learned to craft the riches of the area into products they used everyday. The Indians were great storytellers and the histories of their ancestors were acted out in the campfire light. Four hundred years ago, the elders began to speak of strange new people arriving in ships with sails as white as their skin. The new people from Europe lived very differently than the Native Americans. They saw the land and forest of the Great Lakes region as theirs for the taking. In a short time, the natives lost their Great Lakes home to people from other lands, and the forests were cut to make way for the modern world.

Precambrian
Copper and iron found in the Lake Superior region were carried to the surface in the lava of ancient volcanoes.

Lake Superior

Great Lakes Bedrock

Precambrian

Cambrian

Ordovician

Silurian

Devonian

Carboniferous

Lake Michigan

Carboniferous
Coal and oil are formed deep in the earth from layers of buried forest. Coal melts iron to steel. Oil feeds our hungry cars.

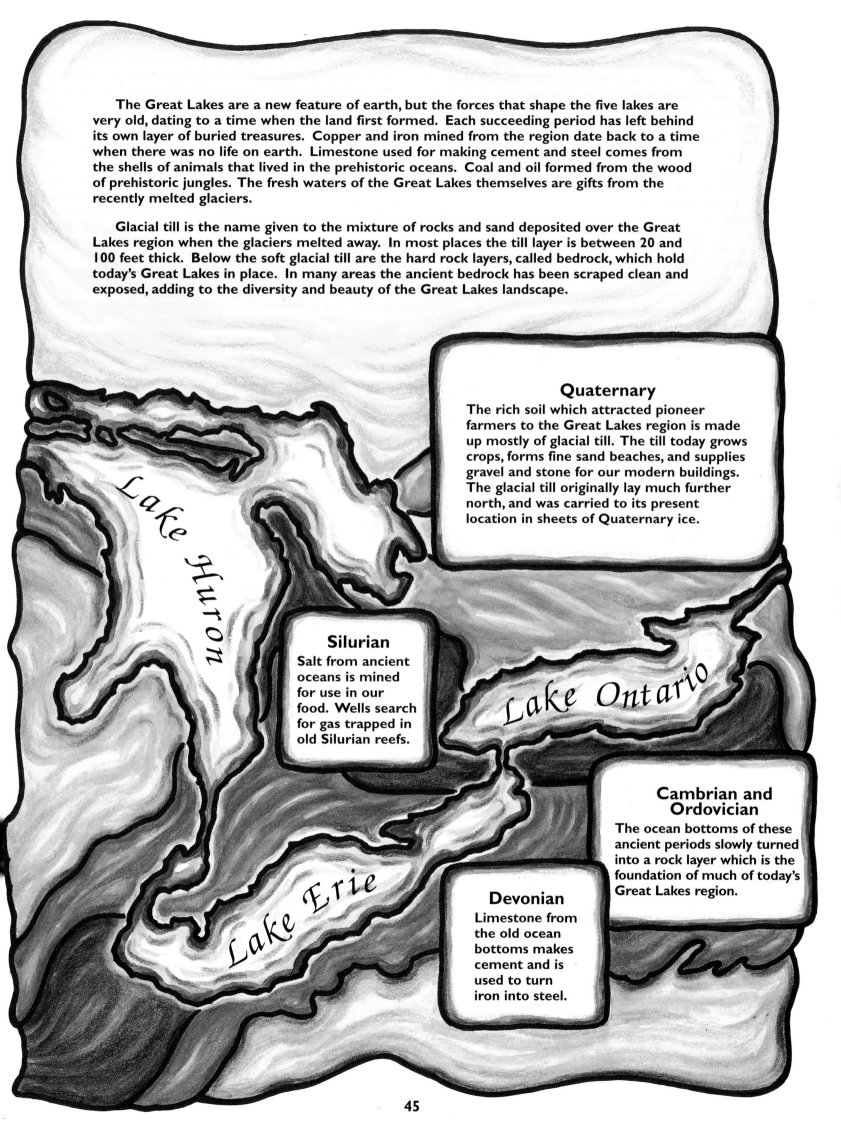

The Great Lakes are a new feature of earth, but the forces that shape the five lakes are very old, dating to a time when the land first formed. Each succeeding period has left behind its own layer of buried treasures. Copper and iron mined from the region date back to a time when there was no life on earth. Limestone used for making cement and steel comes from the shells of animals that lived in the prehistoric oceans. Coal and oil formed from the wood of prehistoric jungles. The fresh waters of the Great Lakes themselves are gifts from the recently melted glaciers.

Glacial till is the name given to the mixture of rocks and sand deposited over the Great Lakes region when the glaciers melted away. In most places the till layer is between 20 and 100 feet thick. Below the soft glacial till are the hard rock layers, called bedrock, which hold today's Great Lakes in place. In many areas the ancient bedrock has been scraped clean and exposed, adding to the diversity and beauty of the Great Lakes landscape.

Quaternary

The rich soil which attracted pioneer farmers to the Great Lakes region is made up mostly of glacial till. The till today grows crops, forms fine sand beaches, and supplies gravel and stone for our modern buildings. The glacial till originally lay much further north, and was carried to its present location in sheets of Quaternary ice.

Silurian

Salt from ancient oceans is mined for use in our food. Wells search for gas trapped in old Silurian reefs.

Cambrian and Ordovician

The ocean bottoms of these ancient periods slowly turned into a rock layer which is the foundation of much of today's Great Lakes region.

Devonian

Limestone from the old ocean bottoms makes cement and is used to turn iron into steel.

The inventor Henry Ford was smart to chose the heart of the Great Lakes region as the place to build his cars. For in addition to his vision and skills, the natural resources he needed to manufacture cars on a large scale were abundant in the area. A thousand pounds of iron went into every Model T car. Coal fired the furnaces that turned iron to steel. Limestone was ground down and mixed into cement to build factories and roads. Fleets of ships crisscrossed the big lakes carrying anything from iron to finished cars to ports along the Great Lakes, and beyond.

The people of the Great Lakes continue to use the resources laid down over the ages to create the metal treasures of our modern world. Today the region is a manufacturing center whose industry and products are responsible for much of North America's wealth.

We humans are the first earthly creatures to see ourselves within the framework of time. All other plants and animals experience the beauty and hazards of life on a moment to moment basis. Our understanding of the world is more complex. We know we live on the front edge of time, the latest chapter in the story of our ancient earth.

The grand lesson of history is that things are always changing, from the face of the earth to the face of life itself. For now, we share a great moment in time, a story in progress. New discoveries will continue to define and enrich our knowledge of the past, while new generations will carry us forward to face the changes and challenges of the 21st century.